TEN STEPS TO BUILD AND BE SPIRIT FILLED

Learn to Receive the Holy Spirit in Ten Steps

By Dr. Harry Assad Salem III

Illustrations by Kay Horn

Unless otherwise indicated, all Scripture quotations are taken from the *King James® Bible and the English Standard® Bible.* Copyright © 1982 by Thomas Nelson, Inc. Used by permission.

LEARNING PALS TEN STEPS TO BUILD AND BE SPIRIT FILLED
ISBN 1-890370-40-1

Copyright © 2018 by Salem Family Ministries

Salem Family Ministries
PO Box 1595
Cathedral City, CA 92234
www.salemfamilyministries.org

No part of this book may be reproduced or transmitted in any form or by any means, electronic or mechanical, including photocopying, recording, or by any information storage and retrieval system, without permission in writing from Salem Family Ministries.

Disclaimer: The views expressed in this book contain personal opinions, theories, and experiences throughout life and time spent in God's word and private research. They are expressed as opinion and views only, and are shared with you from lifelong experience and research. They are only communicated to you from personal study and research.

-INTRODUCTION-

"RECEIVING THE HOLY SPIRIT"

The Holy Spirit is God's helper on earth. Jesus operated in ministry through the application of the Holy Spirit while He was on the earth. The Holy Spirit is a teacher that teaches mankind how to live, how to have a good life, and how to have relationship with God. When we receive the Holy Spirit, then we can have greater relationship with God as we are choosing to let the same helper who helped Jesus perform miracles take control of our own lives. This means we are letting God lead us and help us to live and be happy through the Holy Spirit.

We are showing God we love Him by doing what His Holy Spirit tells us, and how He leads us. When children receive the Holy Spirit they can grow up on a more fulfilled and happy pace. John 14:26 ESV says, *"But the Helper, the Holy Spirit, whom the Father will send in My name, He will teach you all things and bring to your remembrance all that I have said to you."* Let us now learn how to build relationship and receive the Holy Spirit in our lives in ten easy steps.

GOD made all life.

GOD built it with His hands.

GOD gave us His Holy Spirit

The Holy Spirit helps us build
with our hands.

How do we accept the Holy Spirit?

We do it by building relationship.

Relationship is loving
and accepting people in our hearts.

Let's build relationship with the Holy Spirit in ten steps.

Step one, we say, "Dear Father GOD."

Step two, we say,
"We love you, GOD."

Step three, we ask to learn from GOD's Holy Spirit.

Step four, we ask to receive the Holy Spirit.

Step five, we ask the Holy Spirit into our hearts.

Step six, we ask to build relationship with the Holy Spirit.

Step seven we accept the Holy Spirit in our hearts.

Step eight, we ask to learn prayer language, also called "tongues."

Step nine, we now have relationship with the Holy Spirit.

Step ten, we say, "Yahoo!" as we now have learned how to build and be spirit-filled.

CLOSING AND GRATITUDE

Thank you for reading today. I hope that you enjoyed learning how to build relationship and be filled with the Holy Spirit. Developing a relationship involving the Holy Spirit is a vital key to having an excellent relationship with God. It is a way to walk in fulfillment with God and show Him that we love Him. A relationship with the Holy Spirit at a young age can further develop a more complete spiritual walk into adulthood and teach a child the value of relationship.

Children today need to be taught how to love people, how to be loved, and what kind of love should be reflected in their hearts. A relationship with the Holy Spirit will instill lessons of love and relationship in a child's spirit, mind, and heart that will better help them understand how to use those gifts in relationships with others. It will bring them a greater sense of joy, fulfillment, and completion.

Accepting the Holy Spirit at a young age will help develop a person's prayer language. Prayer language or tongues is the private language that people can talk to God with and learn lessons from God that are special and reserved privately for God and those He loves. God desires intimacy with His children. The Holy Spirit can help make such a relationship between God and His children a reality.

ABOUT THE AUTHOR

Dr. Harry Assad Salem III is an author of several books dealing with theology, archaeology, religion, history, and science. He holds state, regional, national, and world championships in the sports of powerlifting and strongman. He is also an NPC bodybuilder.

Dr. Salem holds five doctorate degrees in the fields of theology, archaeology, Biblical studies, Christian education, and practical ministry. He has been involved in ministry since the age of thirteen with Salem Family Ministries. He has lectured at School of Worship for several years. He has developed a children's book series called Prayer Buddies with two books published called Count of Ten Say Amen and Ten Steps to Build and be Spirit Filled.

Dr. Salem is an advocate of education who believes that the highest goals one can achieve can be reached through knowledge and skills learned in the classroom or on the job, and applied in the world to gain experience and mastery over anything and everything. Dr. Salem's personal motto and creed is, "Excellence is excellent." It is a belief that has kept him thriving for the highest of excellence in every pursuit he has worked towards. He hopes to inspire others to achieve their own pursuits of excellence, foster climates of change in their lives, and live to their fullest potential in everyway possible. He has one niece, Mia Gabrielle Salem, and one nephew, Roman Harry Salem Jr.

I would love to hear from you. There are many ways to stay connected to me. You can contact me either through the mail or the internet at the ministry website.

Salem Family Ministries

P.O. Box 1595

Cathedral City, CA 92234

www.salemfamilyministries.org